2/02   ◦ 216

W9-BTM-689

DATE DUE

DEMCO 128-8155

Great African Americans

Marian Anderson.

a great singer

Revised Edition

Patricia and Fredrick McKissack

Series Consultant
Dr. Russell L. Adams, Chairman
Department of Afro-American Studies, Howard University

Enslow Publishers, Inc.

40 Industrial Road   PO Box 38
Box 398   Aldershot
Berkeley Heights, NJ 07922   Hants GU12 6BP
USA   UK

http://www.enslow.com

For Mrs. Evelyn Glore-Ashford

Revised edition of Marian Anderson: A Great Singer © 1991

Library of Congress Cataloging-in-Publication Data

McKissack, Pat, 1944–
    Marian Anderson: a great singer / Patricia and Fredrick McKissack. —Rev. ed.
        p. cm. — (Great African Americans)
    Summary: Tells the story of the African-American singer who struggled against prejudice to become one of the great opera performers of the century.
    Includes index.
    ISBN 0-7660-1676-5
    1. Anderson, Marian, 1897–1993—Juvenile literature. 2. Contraltos—United States—Biography—Juvenile literature. [1. Anderson, Marian, 1897–1993. 2. Singers. 3. Women—Biography.
4. Afro-Americans—Biography.]
    I. McKissack, Fredrick. II. Title.
    ML3930.A5 M4   2001
    782.1′092—dc21

                         00-012149

Printed in the United States of America

10 9 8 7 6 5 4 3 2 1

To Our Readers: We have done our best to make sure all Internet addresses in this book were active and appropriate when we went to press. However, the author and the publisher have no control over and assume no liability for the material available on those Internet sites or on other Web sites they may link to. Any comments or suggestions can be sent by e-mail to comments@enslow.com or to the address on the back cover.

Every effort has been made to locate all copyright holders of material used in this book. If any errors or omissions have occurred, corrections will be made in future editions of this book.

Illustration Credits: Historical Society of Pennsylvania, p. 7T; Library of Congress, pp. 7B, 11, 19, 26; Marian Anderson Collection of Photographs, Rare Book & Manuscript Library, University of Pennsylvania, pp. 6, 7, 8, 9, 10B, 11, 12, 14, 15, 18, 20, 24, 26; Musical Fund Society of Philadelphia Records, Rare Book & Manuscript Library, University of Pennsylvania, p. 10T; National Archives, p. 22; Laura Wheeling Waring (1887–1948), oil on canvas, National Portrait Gallery, Smithsonian Institution, p. 17; Photographs and Prints Division, Schomburg Center for Research in Black Culture/The New York Public Library/Astor Lenox and Tilden Foundation, pp. 3, 4, 23, 25; United Nations, p. 27.

Cover Illustrations: Marian Anderson Collection of Photographs, Rare Book & Manuscript Library, University of Pennsylvania; National Archives; Photographs and Prints Division, Schomburg Center for Research in Black Culture/The New York Public Library/Astor Lenox and Tilden Foundation; United Nations.

TABLE OF CONTENTS

Marian Anderson
February 27, 1897–April 8, 1993

CHAPTER 1

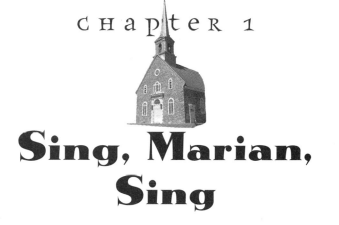

Sing, Marian, Sing

marian Anderson was born February 27, 1897. Her father sold coal in the winter and ice in the summer. Her mother cleaned houses. The Andersons went to church every Sunday.

Mr. Robinson was in charge of the children's choir at Union Baptist Church. He invited Marian to join the choir. She was just six years old. And so began her love of music.

Marian grew up singing in church. She learned

One-year-old Marian.

Marian grew up at 762 Martin Street, left, a row house in Philadelphia. Her father sold coal and ice at the market inside the Reading Terminal, below, a train station in Philadelphia.

the old slave songs called spirituals. She sang alone and with others. Music filled her with happiness. Singing was almost as wonderful as going to the circus . . . almost.

One day, Marian heard music coming from a window. She peeked inside. A dark-skinned woman was playing a piano in her living room. Marian was excited. She felt proud to see a woman who

7

had dark skin like hers playing so beautifully. Marian knew then that if she wanted to, she could learn to play the piano, too.

Marian's family was poor. When her father died, they became even poorer. But Marian didn't mind working. She scrubbed her neighbor's front steps for a penny or two. She sang all the time. Her neighbors loved to hear her sing as she worked.

Marian, center, with her mother and sisters, Alyce, left, and Ethel, right.

8

CHAPTER 2

Mi-Mi-Mi-Mi-Mi-Mi-Mi

arian and her sisters, Alyce and Ethel, played together and went to school together. When they were in high school, they began wondering what they would do when they were grown up. Would they be doctors? Lawyers? Teachers, as their mother once had been?

More than anything else, Marian wanted to sing. But could a poor, black girl from Philadelphia sing well enough to make a living? Yes, she decided, it was possible.

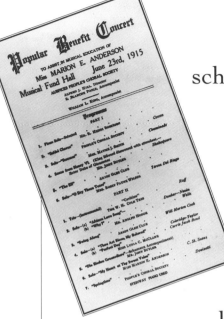

Marian went to a nearby music school. She could hear singing.

Mi-Mi-Mi-Mi-Mi-Mi-Mi

"What do *you* want? We don't teach colored people," a woman told Marian. "Go away!"

The words were unkind and mean. Marian felt bad—not for herself, but for the woman. How could a person love music and be so filled with hate? she thought.

At last, Marian found someone who was willing to teach her—Mary Saunders Patterson, her first voice teacher. Marian worked hard at her lessons. Soon she

A special concert was held to raise money for Marian's singing lessons.

The first time Marian sang for teacher Giuseppe Boghetti, right, the beauty of her voice made him cry.

was singing her scales.

One day, Marian had a chance to sing for Giuseppe Boghetti, who was a very well known music teacher. He was too busy to take a new student. "But I will listen to her sing," he said. Marian sang "Deep River" for him.

Marian, age twenty-one, sang in a concert at the Philadelphia Academy of Music.

Then, after hearing Marian sing, Boghetti smiled. He said she had a lot of talent. Boghetti said he would take one more student: Marian Anderson.

"The more
I sang,
the more
confident
I became,"
said Marian.

CHAPTER 3

High and Low Times

marian had happy times and sad times in her life. One bad time came in 1924, when she was twenty-seven years old.

Marian studied very hard with Boghetti. She had sung at churches in Philadelphia. Her voice was strong. She was good—very good. Everybody said so. Why not sing in New York?

Boghetti said she would need to work even harder to be ready.

Marian liked the idea of singing in a big music

13

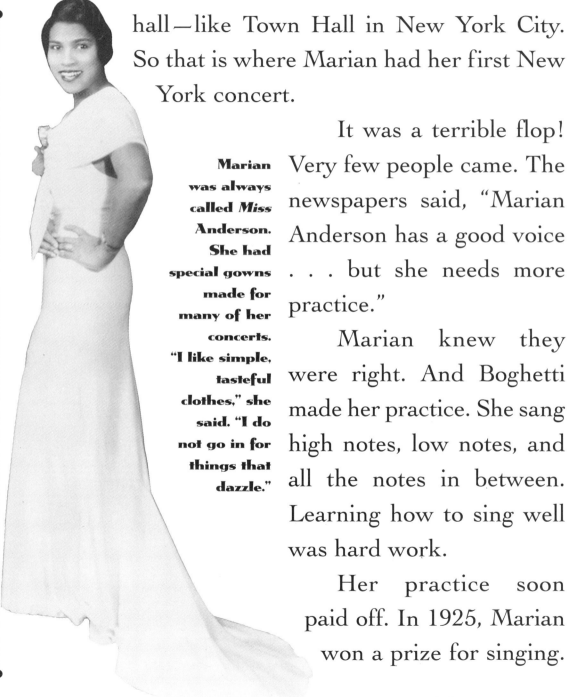

hall—like Town Hall in New York City. So that is where Marian had her first New York concert.

Marian was always called *Miss* Anderson. She had special gowns made for many of her concerts. "I like simple, tasteful clothes," she said. "I do not go in for things that dazzle."

It was a terrible flop! Very few people came. The newspapers said, "Marian Anderson has a good voice . . . but she needs more practice."

Marian knew they were right. And Boghetti made her practice. She sang high notes, low notes, and all the notes in between. Learning how to sing well was hard work.

Her practice soon paid off. In 1925, Marian won a prize for singing.

14

She won a chance to sing a solo with the New York Philharmonic Orchestra in August.

She was good—very good. It felt great! She sang the high notes, the low notes, and all the notes in between. She had never sung them better.

Marian sang at churches, colleges, and concert halls. Kosti Vehanen played the piano for many of her concerts.

15

CHAPTER 4

Brava! Brava!

marian went to Europe at the end of 1927. Her first major European concert was in Germany in early 1930. People cheered for her. Brava! Brava! The crowds cheered.

Next Marian sang in Denmark, Sweden, Norway, and Russia. Her voice was better than ever. She was very well known. But not many people in the United States had heard her sing. It was time to come home.

A concert was set for December 30, 1935, at Town Hall in New York City. On the boat trip home,

Miss Anderson sang in hundreds of cities all over the world. She became a star. But she never forgot to thank her family or her church for their help.

Marian was married to Orpheus Fisher (called "King"). They did not have any children.

Marian broke her leg. The show must go on, she told her family and friends.

Only a few people knew her leg was broken. This time Town Hall was full. Marian stood behind the piano. She wore a long, blue dress.

It was very quiet. The music began. Her leg hurt, but Marian sang and sang, and sang! When she was finished, everyone in the great hall burst into cheers.

Marian sang all over the United States. She sang in the South, where laws ruled that black people and white people had to live separately. They could not go to school together, work or play together. They could not sit together on buses or in music halls.

Whenever Marian sang before a crowd in the South, she bowed to the black people first. That

This rest room was for WHITE LADIES ONLY. In the South, Marian saw how laws kept blacks and whites apart. After a while, she refused to sing in places that did not let people of all races sit together.

was her way of showing she cared. It also showed that she was proud of her race. Brava! Brava! They cheered for her.

Marian and her piano player Franz Rupp clasped hands and bowed after a concert at Carnegie Hall in New York.

CHAPTER 5

Oh, What a Morning!

marian sang at the White House for President Franklin D. Roosevelt and First Lady Eleanor Roosevelt. Mrs. Roosevelt also invited Marian's mother to the White House.

Howard University invited Miss Anderson to sing in Washington, D.C., in 1939 at Constitution Hall. But a group called the Daughters of the American Revolution (DAR), who owned the hall, said no black person could sing there.

Marian was sad—not for herself, but for the Daughters of the American Revolution.

Other people were very angry about the way a great American was being treated. One was Mrs. Roosevelt. She quit the DAR to let the world know she didn't like the way Miss Anderson was treated.

Then, on Easter Sunday morning in 1939, Marian Anderson sang in Washington, D.C. Oh, what a morning!

She stood on the steps of the Lincoln Memorial and sang the National Anthem before 75,000 people of all races. As always, a Marian Anderson concert

Marian enjoyed listening to music at her home in Philadelphia.

22

**Marian sang outdoors at the Lincoln Memorial in Washington, D.C.
"There seemed to be people as far as the eye could see," she said.**

ended with the spirituals she learned as a child. She sang "My Soul Is Anchored in the Lord." It was very beautiful. Some people cried.

In her long career, Miss Anderson won many honors and made many records. She sang for crowds all over the world. In 1955, she became the

Marian dreamed of singing with the famous Metropolitan Opera Company. Rudolf Bing, right, was in charge of the "Met." He gave Marian a tour of the beautiful opera house.

first African American to sing a leading part at the well-known Metropolitan Opera in New York City. She also sang at the March on Washington in 1963, where Dr. Martin Luther King, Jr., gave his "I Have a Dream" speech. Oh, what a morning! She even got to sing at Constitution Hall.

A great conductor, Arturo Toscanini, said that

A day to remember: On January 7, 1955, Marian was the first African American to sing a solo at the Met. Her mother, left, was so proud.

In 1939, First Lady Eleanor Roosevelt presented the Spingarn Medal to Marian. This special award is given by the NAACP, a group that works for equal rights for African Americans.

In 1958, President Dwight D. Eisenhower asked Marian to be a delegate to the United Nations. She worked for peace and under-standing all over the world.

Marian had a voice heard once in a hundred years.

Marian Anderson retired on April 19, 1965, after a concert at New York's Carnegie Hall. In February 1993, Marian celebrated her ninety-sixth birthday. In April, she died.

She will be remembered as a person who brought people together through music.

timeline

1897 ~ Born February 27 in Philadelphia, Pennsylvania.

1923 ~ Wins first prize in Philadelphia Philharmonic Society singing contest.

1924 ~ First Town Hall recital in New York City.

1933 ~ Goes to Europe for a two-year concert tour.

1936 ~ Performs at the White House.

1939 ~ Performs at the Lincoln Memorial in Washington, D.C.

1943 ~ Marries Orpheus "King" Fisher.

1955 ~ Is the first African American to sing in a leading role with New York City's Metropolitan Opera Company.

1958 ~ Serves as a delegate to the United Nations.

1963 ~ Receives Presidential Medal of Freedom.

1965 ~ Retires from singing.

1993 ~ Dies on April 8.

1939

1958

1943

WORDS to KNOW

brava—a cheer used at concerts to show the audience is happy with the singer or actor.

choir—A musical group; a group of singers, sometimes in a church.

colored—An outdated name that was used for African Americans.

concert—A musical show.

Daughters of the American Revolution (DAR)—A group of women whose ancestors fought in the Revolutionary War.

delegate—A person chosen to speak or act for someone else or for a group. Marian was a delegate to the United Nations. She spoke for the United States.

national anthem—The song of a country. The national anthem of the United States is "The Star-Spangled Banner."

National Association for the Advancement of Colored People (NAACP)—An organization started to help all Americans gain equal rights and protection under the law. The NAACP is one of the oldest civil rights organizations in the United States.

WORDS TO KNOW

note—A musical sound; a music symbol that shows the musician what sound to make. When put together, notes make music.

philharmonic orchestra—A large group of musicians who play concerts for audiences.

practice—To go over and over something until it is learned well.

president—The leader of a country or group.

race—A group of people who all share the same ancestors.

retired —To stop working.

scales—Musical sounds that move higher or lower note by note. Singers practice scales before singing.

spirituals—Religious songs that were first sung by African-American slaves.

student—A person who is interested in learning.

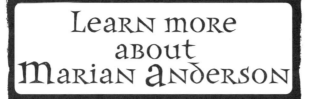
Learn more about Marian Anderson

Books

Broadwater, Andrea. *Marian Anderson: Singer and Humanitarian.* Berkeley Heights, N.J.: Enslow Publishers, Inc., 2000.

Ferris, Jerri. *What I Had Was Singing: The Story of Marian Anderson.* Minneapolis: Carolrhoda Books, Inc., 1994.

Livingston, Myra C. *Keep on Singing: A Ballad of Marian Anderson.* New York, N.Y.: Holiday House, 1994.

Recordings

Marian Anderson: Songs by Schubert and Schumann (BMG/RCA Victor, 2000)

Marian Anderson, Spirituals: He's Got the Whole World (BMG/RCA Victor, 1994)

Internet Addresses

Marian Anderson: A Life in Song
Photos, sound clips, and more.
<http://www.library.upenn.edu/special/gallery/anderson/index.html>

Marian Anderson Biography
<http://www.afrovoices.com/anderson.html>

Marian Anderson
<http://www.worldbook.com/fun/aamusic/html/anderson2.htm>

Index